OUTLAW KARATE:

THE SECRET OF THE ONE YEAR BLACK BELT

Al Case

AL CASE

QUALITY PRESS

For information regarding this book contact:

MonsterMartialArts.com
or
AlCaseBooks.com

ISBN-13: 978-1495421433

ISBN-10: 1495421430

To think you are the only one right
is the surest way to invite a fight
the True Way is to make others right
that is an art that is filled with might

ACKNOWLEDGEMENTS

Josh Valenti (1st black-Outlaw Karate)
Ron Grim (1st black-Outlaw Karate)
Fred Pfiefle (1st black-Tai Chi Chuan)
Paul Pfiefle (1st black-Tai Chi Chuan)
Wes Dick (1st black-Tai Chi Chuan)
Eddie Doty (2nd black-Outlaw Karate, Ju Jitsu)
Aaron Case (2nd black-Outlaw Karate, Kwon Bup)
Nelson Webb (2nd black-Matrix Karate, Monkey Boxing)
Tracy Baron (3rd black-Outlaw Karate, Kwon Bup Karate)
Doug Anderson (3rd black-Kang Duk Won)
Tom Mann (3rd black-Kang Duk Won, Kwon Bup)
Harry Hsu (5th black-Outlaw Karate, Kang Duk Won, Kwon Bup, Monkey Boxing, Tai Chi Chuan, Pa Kua Chang)
Richard Armington (6th black-Outlaw Karate, Fut Ga Shaolin Kung Fu, Tai Chi Chuan, etc.)
Mike Baron (6th black-Outlaw Karate, Monkey Boxing, Kang Duk Won, Kwon Bup, Tai Chi Chuan, Pa Kua Chang, etc.)
Rick Thatcher (7th black-Kang Duk Won, Kwon Bup, Monkey Boxing, Chinese Kenpo, etc.)

THE PURPOSE OF THIS BOOK

1) Undo misconceptions concerning the Martial Arts.

2) Provide a record of research into Martial Methodology.

3) Attain a method by which a True Artist can be created in the shortest possible time.

4) To make sure that, should I return to this planet in another body, I can find the True Art once again.

TABLE OF CONTENTS

INTRODUCTION

The purpose of the Martial Arts is to enable one to survive and to be able to protect those around him. The way to achieve this is to learn how to Analyze and Handle Force and Flow. Thus the Purpose of the Martial Arts is to avoid a Force or Flow while delivering a Force or Flow.

What this all means is that you can't do Karate robotically, merely seeking a good 'Workout.'

Instead, one must analyze how the body works from the inside out. One must actually figure things out.

To enable one to achieve the Purpose of the Martial Arts within Karate I tried many different Forms and arrangements of Forms. Outlaw Karate was the first one I used on a mass scale. I was gratified to find that it worked better than I could have possibly hoped for.

This leads us to an interesting fact. If somebody knows what it is they are trying to do before they do it, they can do it 10x's easier and quicker.

That is the purpose of this book.

1
WHITE BELT

A White Belt is a beginner. The color White implies lack of knowledge. A piece of paper is white before it is written upon.

HOUSE
A beginning Form which replaces all Kebons, and other beginning forms. It presents the basics without any useless moves. When was the last time somebody stepped forward with the right foot and punched you with the right hand? When was the last time you turned 270 degrees into an opponent? These and other irregularities are left out, and the student is shown how to develop a straight line Intention with real life applications, and yet no classical power has been removed. In fact, by creating House I have increased the Classical Power available to a student. I have also decreased the time necessary for a beginner to learn his Basics.

RHYTHMIC FREESTYLE
Most beginners are thrown into freestyle, even introduced to tournaments, as soon as possible. The fact is, how can a person use Karate in a fight before they know it?

Because of this one fact many people join a Karate school and then rapidly quit. Quite simply, they joined to learn how to fight, not to just fight.

To solve this problem I developed Rhythmic Freestyle.

In Rhythmic Freestyle students take turns striking one another slowly. The idea is not to 'Get the point,' but rather to teach one's partner how to block. In this way a student can learn how to apply the knowledge of real Karate to Freestyle without getting beaten up in the process.

Time spent on this level should be about one month, though it will vary depending upon the abilities of the individual learning.

I have to say, at this point, that while I have had great success in the one year program, there have been those who took longer than one year. It really depends on how much of a commitment one is willing to make. A student that practices only in class goes slowly. A student that practices every day can normally achieve Black Belt in a year easily.

2
HOUSE

Ready Position. Stand naturally, feet just past shoulder width apart, body loose but erect, able to move in any direction at any time, without leaning or otherwise giving hint of any direction. A phrase to describe this attitude would be, 'Stand Squarely in the room.'

1

Step back with the left foot into a Back Stance (weight left) and execute a right Low Block.

2

Step forward with the right foot into a Front Stance (weight right) and execute a left Punch.

3

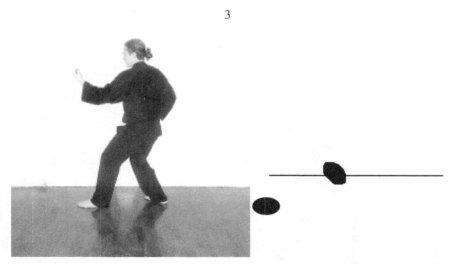

Step forward with the left foot into a Back Stance (weight right) and execute a left Outward Middle Block.

4

Step forward with the left foot into a Front Stance (weight left) and execute a right Punch.

5

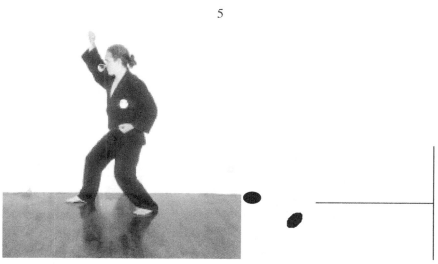

Step forward with the right foot into a Back Stance (weight left) and execute a right High Block.

6

Step forward with the right foot into a Front Stance (weight right) and execute a left Punch. KIAI!

7

Step back with the right foot into an Hourglass Stance facing 90 degrees to the left, and execute a right Upper Cross Palm Block.

3
BASIC/BASICS

To understand a Form one needs to understand what I call the Basic/Basics. These are the underlying building blocks beneath everything in the Martial Arts. It can even be said that an Art that doesn't possess these Concepts is not the True Art.

The way to learn these Concepts is with each one you read go back and apply it to the form, concentrating on that Basic/Basic exclusively.

4
COORDINATED BODY MOTION

Coordinated Body Motion, or CBM, is when all parts of the body move in the same direction at the same time. When the entire body is utilized in this fashion Intention is released. I sometimes express this concept with the phrase, 'One Intention-One Direction.'

To practice CBM one must analyze the body and consciously make it work as One Unit until it does so instinctively and intuitively.

When moving the body begin moving all body parts at the same time. End all motion at the same time.

You must learn to appreciate the mass, weight, size, dimension, and so on of every body part as they relate to every other body part, and to the Whole Body.

THIS CONCEPT IS THE CRUX OF OUTLAW KARATE, AND THE SECRET TO ACHIEVING BLACK BELT IN ONE YEAR!

Go back and do the Form with this concept many times before proceeding.

5
BODY TESTING

Stand in a Front Stance with your arm outstretched and hand in a fist. Have somebody press on your fist. Does your body collapse? At which points does it collapse? This is only a push, what is gong to happen when your fist hits another human being? Simply, can you hold your Form so that your weight is transmitted through your arm (Velocity of punch times weight increases weight upon impact. Think about it.)

The point here is that your body should be tested through every movement of every form so that you learn how to use the Energy of your body.

By Body Testing you learn the proper structural alignment of your body.

By body testing you get stronger in the Karate way, which is developing Energy and Intention.

A good Body Tester will push so that the Energy goes back the arm, down into the Tan Tien, and down the legs.

A good body tester will pull as well as push. This ensures that you gain balance in your Karate.

BODY TESTING IS CRUCIAL TO MAKING YOUR ART ACTUALLY WORK! WITHOUT SUFFICIENT BODY TESTING THE ONE YEAR BLACK BELT WILL BE TOO WEAK!

Go back and do the Form many times with this concept before proceeding.

6
FOCUS

Focus is the concentration of all effort into one moment of time.

Focus is often enhanced by twisting the hands at the end of a strike.

Focus is better enhanced by learning how to 'Snap' the fists closed. This is called 'Loose-Tight.'

Focus of the hands must coincide with the dropping of the weight down the appropriate foot (feet).

Focus should coincide with Breathing outward.

In short, Focus must join all the other concepts and body parts in the search for CBM in your Art.

Go back and do the Form many times with this concept before proceeding.

7
GROUNDING

Grounding is the sinking of one's weight into the ground.

Grounding conducts Energy through the aligned body into the ground.

Grounding establishes a base upon the planet from which you cannot be moved should you not want to be moved.

Grounding establishes a base upon the planet for the launching of a strike.

Sinking the weight into the ground ultimately creates a Two Pole Energy System with the planet.

THE ABILITY TO GROUND IS THE SECRET OF POWER. HE WHO CAN'T BE MOVED, OR WHO POSSESSES THE ABILITY TO MOVE OTHERS, HAS POWER.

Go back and do the Form many times with this concept before proceeding.

8
BREATHING

Always breathe from the Tan Tien (The One Point-The Center of the body). Though air won't physically reach past the lungs, the idea of Energy will. This will cause the Tan Tien to produce Energy, which is then channeled to the various body parts.

Always breathe out when expanding the body, and in when contracting the body.

Always breathe out when striking or when being struck.

Use breathing to channel awareness and Energy into your body parts.

BREATHING ESTABLISHES YOUR BODY AS AN INTEGRATED UNIT.

Go back and do the Form many times with this concept before proceeding.

9
HOUSE APPLICATIONS

There are many more applications to the Forms than I list here. Consider that the body is actually surrounded by a circle of blocks.

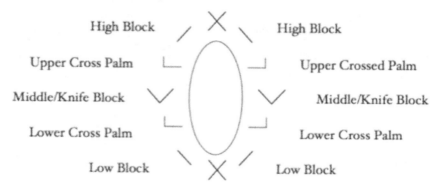

High Crossed Wrist Block

High Block   High Block

Upper Cross Palm   Upper Crossed Palm

Middle/Knife Block   Middle/Knife Block

Lower Cross Palm   Lower Cross Palm

Low Block   Low Block

Low Crossed Wrist Block

Keeping this data in mind move your hands through any form and you will constantly be finding yourself in combinations of these blocks.

I hope this helps you 'Read between the lines.'

The applications for the Form House provide for defense in the directions of up, down, left and right.

LOW BLOCK

The Attacker kicks to the belly with his left leg.

The Defender steps back with the left leg into a Back Stance (weight left) and executes a right Low Block.

The Defender steps forward with the right leg into a Front Stance (weight right) and executes a left punch to the body.

OUTWARD MIDDLE BLOCK

The Attacker steps forward with the left leg and punches to the body with the left hand.

The Defender steps back with the left leg into a Back Stance (weight left) and executes a right Outward Middle Block.

The Defender steps forward with the right leg into a Front Stance (weight right) and executes a left Punch to the body.

HIGH BLOCK

The Attacker steps forward with the right leg and punches to the face with the right hand.

The Defender steps back with the left leg into a Back Stance (weight left) and executes a right High Block.

The Defender steps forward with the right leg into a Front Stance (weight right) and executes a left Punch to the body.

INWARD MIDDLE BLOCK (HAMMER)

The Attacker steps forward with the right leg and punches to the body with the right hand.

The Defender steps back with the left leg into a Back Stance (weight left) and executes a right Inward Middle Block.

The Defender steps forward with the right leg into a Front Stance (weight right) and executes a right Punch to the body.

10
GREEN BELT

A Green Belt is an intermediate student. The color green indicates lush growth.

TEMPLE
I developed Temple out of an Okinawan Form called Giin. The basic blocks and stances are developed further and expanded into eight directions.

If you look at House (on the three lines as I suggested) you will notice that it weaves back and forth. You will notice this concept being taken further in Temple, and in the future forms of Crane and Dart. While there is much to be said for standing in one place and duking it out with somebody, I would prefer to take that slight sidestep which removes me from the angle of attack, and automatically opens the opponent.

TWO STEP RHYTHMIC FREESTYLE
Rhythmic Freestyle is taken a step further on this level. It is called Two Strike, and the idea is to launch two strikes in a row, and to erect two blocks in a row, and thus develop more randomity within the exercise without endangering oneself.

11
TEMPLE

Assume a Natural Stance facing North.

1

Step to the right (East) with the right leg into a Horse Stance. Simultaneously execute a right Low Block and a left Outward Middle Block.

2

Pivot to the left (West) into a Back Stance and execute a right High Block and a left Low Block.

3

Pivot to the right (East) into a Back Stance and execute a left High Block and a right Low Block.

4

Bring the left foot to the right and pivot 135 degrees to the left (Northwest). Assume a Cat Stance (Weight right) and execute a right Upper Cross Palm Block.

5

Step forward with the left leg (Northwest) into a Front Stance and execute a left High Block.

6

Execute a right Punch.

7

Bring the right foot to the left and pivot 90 degrees to the right (Northeast). Assume a Cat Stance (Weight left) and execute a left Upper Cross Palm Block.

8

Step forward with the right foot (Northeast) into a Front Stance and execute a right High Block.

9

Execute a left Punch.

10

Step forward (North) with the left leg into a Toe Up Back Stance. Simultaneously execute a left Outward Middle Block.

11

Step back with the left leg into a Back Stance. Simultaneously execute a left High Knifehand Block and a right Chop to the neck. KIAI!

12

Step left (Northwest) with the right foot 45 degrees. Pivot 180 degrees into a Back Stance (Weight right) (Southeast). Simultaneously execute Outward Blocks with both hands. (Camera Angle changed 180 degrees.)

13

Simultaneously execute a left Front Snap Kick and a left Upper Cross Palm Block. (Camera angle reversed)

14

Step forward with the left leg into a Front Stance and execute a right Punch. (<u>Camera angle reversed</u>)

15

Execute a left Punch. (<u>Camera angle reversed</u>)

16

Step right (Southwest) 90 degrees with the right leg into a left Back Stance. Simultaneously execute Outward Middle Blocks with both hands. (<u>Camera angle reversed</u>)

17

Simultaneously execute a right Front Snap kick and a right Upper Cross Palm Block. (<u>Camera angle reversed</u>)

18

Step forward with the right leg into a Front Stance and execute a left Punch.(Camera angle reversed)

19

Execute a right Punch. (Camera angle reversed)

20

Bring the right leg back 45 degrees (West) into a Back Stance (Weight left). Simultaneously execute an augmented right Outward Middle Block.

21

Move the left leg 90 degrees to the left (South) into a Toe Up Back Stance (weight right). Simultaneously execute an augmented left Outward Middle Block.

22

Spin hop backwards 180 degrees into a Horse Stance. The right foot will replace the left foot, the left foot will replace the right foot. Face East). Simultaneously execute a right Hammerfist. KIAI! (Camera angle changed!)

23

Bring the right foot 90 degrees left (Face North) feet in the same place that position 2 of the Form occupied). Simultaneously execute Low Blocks with each hand.

24

Execute Outward Middle Blocks with each hand.

25

Execute High Blocks with each hand.

26

Lower both hands (Slowly, as if encountering great resistance) Palm Down. Breathe into the Tan Tien as you execute.

Return to beginning or repeat Form.

12
THE THREE LEVELS

There are Three Levels in the Martial Arts.

1) Mechanics
2) Physics
3) Dynamics

Mechanics has to do with making sure the body is strong, healthy, agile, flexible, and so on.

Physics has to do with Flowing Energy through the body, constructing the body so that it can generate or withstand large amounts of Energy. Energy is, according to the dictionary, 'The Capacity for Work.' Work, in the Martial Arts, is oftentimes related to the amount of weight constructed, generated, withstood, and so on, within the various actions of the Art.

Dynamics has to do with finding the Thought behind your Actions. Behind each and every move there must be a specific Thought. If you can realize the exact purpose behind each and every move you do you will soon be able to see the exact Purpose behind every move your opponent makes, oftentimes at the exact moment he has the Thought of what he will do. Think about what this will mean for your timing.

KARATE DEVELOPS INTUITION EMPIRICALLY.

Go back and do your Forms many times with this concept before proceeding.

13
THREE ELEMENTS

FORM is the shape and structure of something. It is also the essential nature of a thing.

It is an idea.

It is an established method of expression or proceeding.

It is an orderly method of arrangement.

It is the plan or design of a work of Art.

FORM APPLICATION is applying the concepts and theories of the Form in order to make them work.

It is theory applied

FREESTYLE is a Free Form of Self Defense. It is a way of approximating combat without endangering the participants.

It is Theory brought as close to real life as possible.

REALLY, ALL THIS HAS TO DO WITH DEVELOPING WITHIN THE INDIVIDUAL THE ABILITY TO 'THINK WITHIN COMBAT.'

It's not about fighting, it's about the empirical procedure to develop combat intuition of that sort that 'analyzes and Handles,' no matter how dire or unpredictable the situation.

Go back and do your Forms many times with each of these concepts before proceeding.

14
ANGLES

Obviously the structural alignment of the body is of great importance when analyzing how a technique works. Here are a few datums to help you out.

There is a triangle from the toe to the heel to the knee. What angles reduce stress? What angles create stress?

There is a triangle between the base of the feet and the Tan Tien. What happens when the angle between the Tan Tien and one foot goes beyond 90 degrees?

A Middle Block should come 45 degrees upward from the Tan Tien.

A High Block should come 45 degrees upward from the shoulders.

Never let the elbow bend less than ninety degrees.

There are a lot more angles. By analyzing and understanding these you will begin to understand others.

THE SECRET OF A GOOD BODY STRUCTURE IS IN THE ANGLES.

Go back and do your Forms many times with this concept before proceeding.

15
THE INJURY FORMULA

As a student learns he becomes more dangerous. This is because power increases before responsibility. To help students understand this, and to protect them from themselves, and to help them learn even faster, I created the following formula.

SPEED PLUS IGNORANCE EQUALS INJURY

Simply, don't go faster than you understand. Speed up only as your knowledge increases.

Above all else, be aware that what hurts for your body can hurt for somebody else's body.

IF YOU DON'T UNDERSTAND THIS YOU WILL BE A DANGER TO YOUR PARTNER AND A DANGER TO YOURSELF. THIS ALONE WILL STOP YOU FROM ACHIEVING THE HIGHER LEVELS OF THE MARTIAL ARTS.

Go back and do your Forms many times with this concept before proceeding.

16
THE RIGHT DISTANCE

There are six specific distances. The first, weapons, is not in the scope of this book.

So the five we concern ourselves with are:

Feet
Hands
Knees
Elbows
Throws

In a fight one must be cognizant of which distance he is at, and select the right weapon for that distance. One doesn't normally kick while grappling, and you wouldn't try to throw a Samurai sword.

This becomes an extremely important datum as the speed of freestyle increases.

LEARN THIS AND YOU WILL UNDERSTAND WHY THERE IS ALWAYS A PERFECT DEFENSE FOR EVERY OFFENSE.

Go back and do your Forms many times with this concept before proceeding.

17
TEMPLE APPLICATIONS

5
MID-LOW

The Attacker steps forward with the right leg and punches to the body with the right hand.

The Defender steps forward and to the side with the right leg into a Horse Stance and simultaneously executes a left Outward Middle Block and a right Hammerfist to the groin.

6
CROSS-HIGH

The Attacker steps forward with the right leg and punches to the face with the right hand.

The Defender steps back with the left leg into a Back Stance and executes a left Upper Cross Palm Block.

The Attacker punches to the face with the left hand.

The Defender executes a right High Block. The Defender steps forward with the right leg into a Front Stance and executes a left Punch to the body.

7
HIGH-CHOP

The Attacker steps forward with the right leg and punches to the body with the right hand.

The Defender steps back with the left leg into a Back Stance and executes a right Inward Middle Block (Hammer Block).

The Attacker punches to the face with the left hand.

The Defender simultaneously executes a right High Block and a left Chop to the throat.

8
SPLIT KICK

The Attacker steps forward with the right leg and pushes at the chest with both hands.

The Defender simultaneously hops back onto his left leg, executes a right Snap kick and Inverted Outward Middle Blocks with both hands.

The Defender steps forward with the right leg into a Front Stance and executes a left Punch to the chest.

The Defender executes a right Punch to the chest.

9
SPINNING ELBOW

The Attacker steps forward with the left leg and punches to the face with his left hand.

The Defender steps forward with the left leg into a narrow hourglass Stance and executes a left Upper Cross Palm Block.

The Defender spins forward into an Hourglass Stance and executes a vertical Elbow Strike to the chest.

10
SPINNING HAMMER

The Attacker steps forward with the right leg and punches to the face with the right hand.

The Defender steps back with the right leg into an Hourglass Stance and executes a left Upper Cross Palm Block.

The Defender 'Pop/spins' backward into a horse Stance and executes a right Hammerfist to the kidneys.

18
GREEN BROWN BELT
(HALF-BROWN BELT)

The student is half way to Brown Belt.

MOON

This form was called Hangetsu in Japan, which means 'Half Moon,' and Seisan in Okinawa, after it's creator. The term 'Half Moon' refers to the semi circular arcs of the hands and the feet within the form.

When the student first learns this Form the teacher pushes gently on him, checking his structure, by the time the student is ready for Brown Belt the instructor is delivering full power punches. The Instructor must be specially trained on how to do this so that the student isn't damaged, and actually learns how to make the body impervious to strikes. DON'T DO THIS WITHOUT A QUALIFIED INSTRUCTOR.

ONE WAY FREESTYLE

This is the last step before the student is allowed full Freestyle. The rules are simple. One student attacks, the other defends. After every engagement students alternate who is the attacker and who is the defender. An attack can last any where from one to a half dozen strikes. The idea is to get the student able to analyze and handle more and faster attacks without losing the technique he has developed in earlier Freestyle.

19
MOON

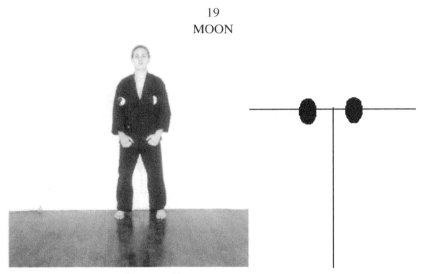

Ready position (face North).

1

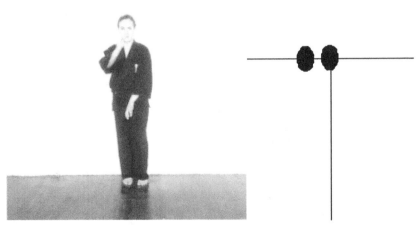

Bring the left foot to the right and execute a left inverted Low Sweep Block and a right Cross Palm Block.

2

Step shoulder width to the left with the left foot a half step and forward into an Hourglass Stance (North). Simultaneously execute a left Outward Middle Block.

3

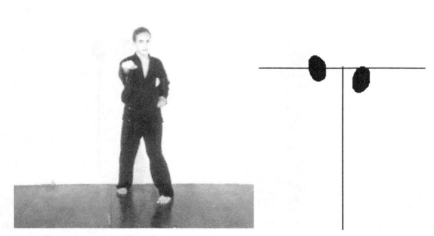

Execute a right Punch.

4

Bring the right foot to the left and execute a right inverted Low Sweep Block and a left Cross Palm Block.

5

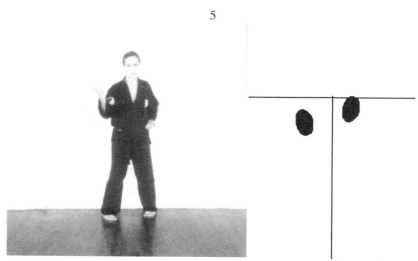

Step shoulder width to the right with the right foot a half step and forward into an Hourglass Stance (North). Simultaneously execute a right Outward Middle Block.

6

Execute a left Punch.

7

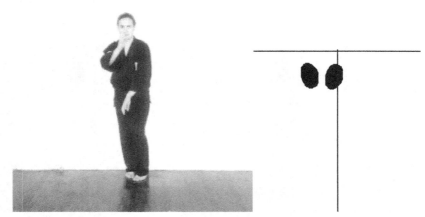

Bring the left foot to the right and execute a left inverted Low Sweep Block and a right Cross Palm Block.

8

Step shoulder width to the left with the left foot a half step and forward into an Hourglass Stance (North). Simultaneously execute a left Outward Middle Block.

9

Execute a right Punch.

10

Execute parries with both hands.

11

Execute single index finger Knuckle Strikes with both hands. KIAI!

12

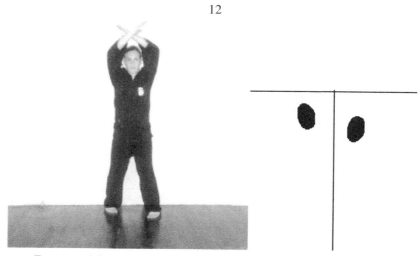

Execute a High Crossed Wrist Block.

13

Execute Low Blocks to the sides with both hands.

14

Step in front of the left foot with the right foot into an Hourglass Stance facing in the opposite direction. Pass the right hand through a Cross Palm Block and simultaneously execute a left Outward Middle Ridgehand Block and a right Low Knifehand Block. (Camera Angle changed 180 degrees.)

15

Filling the arms with great tension move them slowly, as if encountering great resistance, and execute a right Outward Middle Ridgehand Block and a left Low Knifehand Block.

16

Take a Half Moon step forward (South) with the right foot and simultaneously execute a left Outward Middle Ridgehand Block and a right Low Knifehand Block.

17

Filling the arms with great tension move them slowly, as if encountering great resistance, and execute a right Outward Middle Ridgehand Block and a left Low Knifehand Block.

18

Take a Half Moon step forward (South) with the left foot and simultaneously execute a left Outward Middle Ridgehand Block and a right Low Knifehand Block.

19

Filling the arms with great tension move them slowly, as if encountering great resistance, and execute a right Outward Middle Ridgehand Block and a left Low Knifehand Block.

20

Execute parries with both hands.

21

Execute single index finger Knuckle Strikes with both hands. KIAI!

22

Execute a High Crossed Wrist Block.

23

Execute Low Blocks to the sides with both hands.

Turn and repeat form or return to beginning.

20
BASIC ARM POSITIONS

There are only five Basic Arm Positions. These are the most effective way to Flow Energy through the body, any other position is usually only a derivation of these five.

Low (Weight Downward to ground)
Middle (Down 45 degrees to the Tan Tien and then to the ground)
High (Circular and down 45 degrees to the shoulders and down to the Tan Tien and then to the ground)
Circular (Around the shoulders and down to the Tan Tien and then to the ground)
Thrust (Exploding outward from the Tan Tien, which is fixed to the ground)

There are 25 Arm Position combinations. However, 10 are repetitious, so the 15 Basic Arm Positions are:

Low/Low	Mid/Mid	High/Cross
Low/Mid	Mid/High	High/Thrust
Low/High	Mid/Cross	Cross/Cross
Low/Cross	Mid/Thrust	Cross/Thrust
Low/Thrust	High/High	Thrust/Thrust

The trick is to understand these Arm Positions as they relate to hand positions, stances, the way Energy is coursed through the body, and the various trajectories of motion All calculations must be based upon function and resistance.

Go back and do the Forms with this concept many times before proceeding.

21
BASIC ARM GEOMETRIES

The Basic Arm Geometries are the circles and lines described in the transitions of the arms between the five Basic Positions. The Basic Arm Geometries are:

1) Moving up and down
2) Moving side to side
3) Circling clockwise
4) Circling counterclockwise

Combining these geometries will give one an incredible diversity of motion.

The trick is to find and define the purity of the circles and lines through space.

The real trick is to seek CBM through these geometries.

Go back and do the Forms with this concept many times before proceeding.

22
BASIC ARM DIRECTIONS

There are six potential trajectories to enter any arm position.

Up, down, left, right, forward, back.

What this means is that a simple block, such as a right middle block, has six potential ways of being used. For instance:

up-uppercut
down-elbow spike
right-middle block
left-hammer block
forward-backfist
back-pulling

Obviously the blocks will take on different meanings according to trajectory, and will necessitate a study of hand position and stancework. Some trajectories will be usable, some will be very esoteric, and so on.

EXERCISE: Make a list of the Five Arm Positions, make a sub list of the six potentials of motion for each Arm Position, list a usage for each item.

Go back and do the Forms with this concept many times before proceeding.

23
FIXED AND UNFIXED

Just as there are two types of stance, fixed and mobile, moving and unmoving, there are generally two types of forms in Karate. One type of form is moving about, teaching one how to move about while applying the various Martial Arts techniques. The other type is fixed. In this type of Form body motion is not so important as the ability to fix the feet firmly to the mat and generate sufficient power to make the Art work.

Obviously, one should practice both types of Forms.

Go back and do the Forms with this concept many times before proceeding.

24
HARD BODY

When one does Karate the intent is to drop the weight, explode the Energy from the Tan Tien, and channel the Energy through the body to the body part being used for blocking and striking. CBM should be used to make this concept really work.

However, what about when one gets struck? One must then sink the weight, explode the Energy from the Tan Tien, and channel it into the body part being struck.

Moon is fantastic for helping a student do this. In the beginning have a person push sideways on you, Body Test you, so that the Energy is channeled through the body and into the ground. After you are firm in this, and understand all the various ways you can channel Energy, have the person lightly strike you. As time goes on have the strikes increase in power until you are taking full strikes to the body. Obviously you want to make sure the person who is striking you has a full knowledge of the mechanics of Body Testing, and you want to avoid hitting body parts that aren't sufficiently prepared. Also, you want to take your time in doing this exercise. There is much potential for danger here.

Go back and do the Forms with this concept many times before proceeding.

25
MOON APPLICATIONS

11
CROSS OUT

The Attacker steps forward with the right leg as he punches to the face with the right hand.

The Defender assumes an hourglass Stance as he executes a left Cross Palm Block.

The Attacker strikes to the body with the left hand.

The Defender executes a right Outward Middle Block.

The Defender executes a left Punch to the body.

12
WRIST TWIST

The Attacker steps forward with his left foot as he punches to the face with his left hand.

The Defender simultaneously executes a left Front Snap Kick to the belly and a left Cross Palm Block.

The Defender executes a Wrist Twist as he steps back with the left leg.

13
DOUBLE KNUCKLE

The Attacker steps forward with the right leg as he pushes to the chest with both hands.

The Defender assumes an Hourglass Stance as he executes a double Parry.

The Defender executes double Foreknuckles to the pressure points just under and outside the nipples.

14
CROSS PULL

The Attacker steps forward with the left leg as he punches to the face with the left hand.

The Defender assumes an Hourglass Stance as he executes a High Crossed Wrist block.

The Defender executes double Low Blocks to the sides. His left hand pulls the Attacker's left wrist causing the Attacker to fall forward into a rising left knee.

15
CROSS LOCK

The Attacker steps forward with the left leg as he punches to the face with his left hand.

The Defender steps back with the left leg into a Back Stance as he executes a High Crossed Wrist Block.

The Defender steps into a Horse Stance as he pulls the Attacker's wrist with the left hand and presses on the Attacker's elbow with the right forearm, thus executing an Armbar.

16
SPLITTING

The Attacker steps forward with the left leg as he punches to the face with the left hand.

The Defender steps back with the left leg into a Back Stance as he executes a High Crossed Wrist Block.

The Defender steps behind the Attacker's left leg with his right leg, pulls the Attacker's arm down with his left hand as he extends his arm across the Attacker's chest (neck) in a takedown.

17
LOW-MID

The Attacker front kicks to the belly with the left leg.

The Defender steps back with the right leg into a Back Stance as he executes a right Low Knifehand Block and a left Outward Middle Ridgehand Block.

The Attacker sets his foot forward and punches to the face with the right hand.

The Defender executes a left Low Knifehand Block and a right Outward Middle Ridgehand Block.

The Defender pulls the Attacker's arm down with his right hand as he executes a left Spear Hand to the throat.

26
3RD BROWN BELT

A White Belt is dangerous because he doesn't know what he is doing.
A Green Belt is dangerous because he is filled with vim and vigor.
But a Brown Belt is the most dangerous because he has Power.
A Black Belt isn't very dangerous because he can control the Power.
So remember that as you go through the Brown Belt Levels. Search for Control. Control is the Art, not the Power you are so joyfully wielding.

The Material for the 2nd Brown Belt is the Form Crane. Crane followed somewhat the same footwork as the Form Temple. In it you will find techniques from Kang Duk Won Forms called Pinans (Peaceful Mind) and No-Hai (Vision of a White Heron?)

I created the Form with Classical Technique and Power in mind, but none of the confusions or repetitions of the classical forms.

27
CRANE

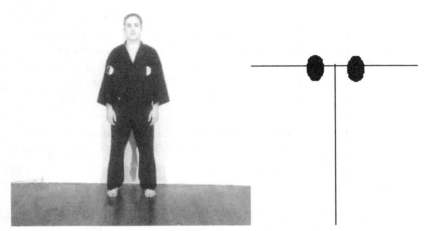

Ready Position. (Stand Natural facing North.)

1

Step to the right (East) into a horse Stance. Simultaneously execute a left, open handed Low Block to the left.

2

Execute a right, open handed Outward Middle Block to the right (West).

3

Execute a left, open handed High Block to the left (East).

4

Retract your right leg and pivot into a Back Stance (weight left) facing to the right (East). Simultaneously execute a right Single Knife Block.

5

Execute a left Punch (East).

6

Bring the left foot to the right and pivot 135 degrees to the left (Northwest). Retract both hands to the waist.

7

Step forward (Northwest) with the left foot. Hook the right foot behind the knee (Crane Stance). Simultaneously execute a right Low Block and a left High Block.

8

Step to the right (Northeast) with the right leg. As you fall execute a left Cross Palm Block.

9

Land in a Front Stance (Northeast) with the right leg (Weight right). Execute a right Chop as you land.

10

Execute a left Punch.

11

Hook the left foot behind the knee (Crane Stance). Simultaneously execute a left Low Block and a right High Block.

12

Step to the left (Northwest) with the left leg. As you fall execute a right Cross Palm Block.

13

Land in a Front Stance (Northwest) with the left leg (Weight left). Execute a left Chop as you land.

14

Execute a right Punch.

15

Move the right leg to the North and the left leg to the South. Face north in a Back Stance (Weight left). Simultaneously execute a right Low Block and a left High Block.

16

Pivot 180 degrees (South) and assume a Back Stance (weight right). Simultaneously execute a left Low Block and a right High Block. (Change of camera angle.)

17

Step forward and to the left (Southeast) with the left leg into a Front Stance (weight left). Simultaneously execute a right Low Block to the right (Southwest) and a left High Block.

18

Bring the right leg up to the right in a Cat Stance (weight left) facing Southwest. Simultaneously execute a right Reverse Low Block and a left Slanted Cross Palm Block.

19

Execute a left Parry and a right Backfist and a right Snap Kick to the Southwest.

20

Step forward (Southwest) with the right leg into a Front Stance (weight right) and execute a left Horizontal Elbow to the right hand.

21

Execute a left Low Block (Southeast) and a right High Block.

22

Bring the left leg up to the right in a Cat Stance (weight right) facing Southeast. Simultaneously execute a left Reverse Low Block and a right Slanted Cross Palm Block.

23

Execute a right Parry and a left Backfist and a left Snap Kick to the southeast.

24

Step forward (Southeast) with the left leg into a Front Stance (weight left) and execute a right Horizontal Elbow to the right hand.

25

Replacement Hop to the right approximately 180 degrees (So that you face North) into a Horse Stance as you execute a right Hammer Fist to the right (East). (Change of camera angle.)

Repeat form or return to the beginning position.

28
HURTS SO GOOD

Pain hurts.

There are two types of pain. There is the pain that says the body is damaged, or in danger of being damaged. One must always pay attention to this kind of pain.

Then there is the kind of pain that is just a lazy body protesting work. This kind of pain must always be ignored.

I'm going to tell you something that normal people don't know, and which a person without the requisite experience would shake their head and say is insane.

After a while pain feels sort of good. It sort of wakes you up, vitalizes you, even gives a sort of a rush.

This is called being in charge of the pain, instead of letting the pain be in charge of you.

A White Belt learns that pain hurts.

A Green Belt learns that pain can be withstood.

A Brown Belt learns that pain can be enjoyed.

A Black Belt learns that pain hurts others.

A Master learns that pain can benefit others.

Pain, after all, is not what life is really all about.

The Martial Arts are what life is all about.

Go back and do the Forms with this concept many times before proceeding.

29
YOU CAN'T FIGHT
WHAT YOU CAN'T FACE

You can't fight what you can't face.

Never blink unduly. Don't flinch, no matter what is happening. It's hard to stare at a fist coming at your face. It's hard to look somebody in the eye when they are trying to hurt you. But look at it this way. if you take your eyes off the action you will get hit anyway. You might just as well see what is happening. This is better than not seeing and having it happen. After all, if you can look and see the chances of mounting an adequate defense are enhanced. After a while if you keep practicing, if you keep forcing yourself to perceive that which is fast and furious, you will find that it is not quite as fast and furious as you thought it was, and you won't get hit. The trick is to just keep your eyes open and your awareness extended at all times.

The fact that Martial Artists force themselves to face that which is not necessarily enjoyable, the fist in the face, the hard block, a little extra pain, is what makes them a little better than those who can't face such things.

Go back and do the Forms with this concept many times before proceeding.

30
WHAT KARATE IS

There is specialization in the Martial Arts.
Aikido specializes in Flowing Throws.
Judo specializes in Force Throws.
Kung Fu specializes in Explosive Circles.
Karate specializes in explosive lines.

Of course, any Art can be evolved out of any other Art. So regardless of the specialization of a particular Art, the door to all Arts eventually opens. The trick is to do a motion enough times that you can see the other options. When you can you will see that Karate has soft circles, and hard throws and all manner of other geometries.

There is a permeation of the Soul by the Art. The Soul realigns according to the Art. There is a Truth of Self that must manifest. The only way to think on this is that without yourself there is no Art. Or, to state it more succinctly...You are the Art.

31
THE SECRET OF POWER

The Secret of Power is space.

Consider, the sun is bright, but it wouldn't be so bright if it wasn't in the middle of Space.

Consider a candle in a coal mine.

What makes these objects bright, regardless of the wattage put out, is the fact that they are in the middle of darkness, of space, of Space.

So when you strike, before you strike you must create Space in your mind. You do this by relaxing every body part until there is no hint of motion to come. Practice your Forms taking long seconds, even minutes, between moves, and between every move practice relaxing. Relax until you virtually forget what it is you are going to do. Only when you achieve this type of relaxation on a permanent basis will your technique explode in purity.

Go back and do the Forms with this concept many times before proceeding.

32
WHAT YOU DON'T KNOW

Life can be divided into two areas, what you know and what you don't know.

It is easy to rely on what you know, to fall into familiar patterns and easy routines.

It is difficult to go forward into what you don't know.

But consider everything that you know as being the flat of a table that you stand upon. And consider everything beyond the table darkness. Your duty is, whenever you see darkness beyond the flat of the table, to take a step outward and, thereby, to enlargen the table of what you know.

A True Martial Artist makes a practice, every time he sees something that he doesn't know, of going forward.

After a while the table of what you know becomes larger than the darkness of what you don't know.

Go back and do the Forms with this concept many times before proceeding.

33
CRANE APPLICATIONS

18
CB PULL

The Attacker steps forward with the right leg and punches to the face with the right hand.

The Defender steps back with the left leg and executes a right Single Knife Hand Block.

The Defender grabs the Attacker's arm and, sinking his weight into his left leg, he pulls the Attacker to him as he executes a left punch.

19
FALLING CRANE

The Attacker kicks to the groin with the left leg.

The Defender lifts his right leg and assumes a Crane Stance while simultaneously executing a right Low Block and a left High Block.

The Attacker, placing his left foot forward, punches to the face with his left hand.

The Defender steps forward with the right leg. As he moves into the opponent he executes a left Cross Palm Block. Simultaneously he prepares his right hand.

The Defender assumes a Front Stance (Weight right) and strikes across the throat with a right Chop.

20
HORSE PUNCHING

The Attacker steps forward with the right leg and punches to the face with the right hand.

The Defender executes a right leg raise (the instep of the foot being utilized) into the Attacker's groin while executing a left Cross Palm Block.

The Defender brings the right foot down to sink his weight into a Horse Stance while executing a right Punch to the body.

21
REVERSE HIP THROW

The Attacker steps forward with the right leg and punches to the face with his right hand.

The Defender cross steps with his right foot to the outside of the Attacker's foot. Simultaneously he executes a left Cross Palm Block.

The Defender thrust his right leg between the Attacker's legs so that he is in a Front Stance facing ninety degrees from the angle of attack. His right leg knocks the Attacker's leg away. Simultaneously he executes a right grab to the throat. This forces the Attacker over the leg in a Takedown.

22
ROLLING BACKFIST

The Attacker steps forward with the right foot and punches to the face with the right hand.

The Defender simultaneously executes a left Parry and a right Front Snap Kick (Stopping the Attacker) and a right Vertical Backfist to the bridge of the nose.

The Defender steps forward with the right leg into a Front Stance (weight right) an as he executes a left horizontal Elbow to the chest.

23
SPINNING SIDE KICK

The Attacker steps forward with the right foot and punches to the face with the right hand.

The Defender steps back with the left leg into a Back Stance as he executes a left Cross Palm Block.

The Defender replaces his right foot with his left foot, while spinning to the rear and executing a right Side thrust Kick. The feet should impact upon the ground and the opponent simultaneously.

34
2ND BROWN BELT

The material for the First Brown Belt is in the Form called Fort.

In Karate there are two schools of thought. One calls for mobility, the other for solidity. I teach Mobility through the Forms of Temple, Crane and Dart. I teach solidity through the Forms of Hourglass (a very simplified form for children), Moon and Fort.

35
FORT

Ready position-Stand natural with feet shoulder width apart (North).

1

0

Step back (South) with the left foot into a Back Stance (Weight left). Simultaneously swing the right hand up and clockwise in a circle to an Inverted Low Sweeping Block, and swing the left hand down and clockwise in a circle to a Cross Palm Block.

2

Step forward (North) with the right foot into a Front Stance (Weight right) and execute a right Punch.

3

Bring the left foot up to an Hourglass Stance (North) and execute a right, Augmented Upper Middle Knife Edge Block.

4

Step back (South) with the right foot into a Back Stance (weight right). Simultaneously execute a left Knife Edge Low Block. The right hand should be open, palm up, at the waist.

5

Step forward (North) with the right foot into an Hourglass Stance. The left toes should be on a line with the middle of the right foot. Simultaneously execute a Double Over/Under Punch. The right fist should be on top of the left fist (6 inches), and both fists should be vertical.

6

Circle both hands in a clockwise manner. Slide through a left Cross Palm Block on the way to a right Outward Middle Block.

7

Execute a right Upper Cross Palm Block and a left Punch.

8

Step forward (North) with the left foot into an Hourglass Stance. The right toes should be on a line with the middle of the left foot. Simultaneously execute a Double Over/Under Punch. The left fist should be on top of the right fist (6 inches), and both fists should be vertical.

9

Circle both hands in a counter clockwise manner. Slide through a right Cross Palm Block on the way to a left Outward Middle Block.

10

Execute a left Upper Cross Palm Block and a right Punch.

11

Step forward (North) with the right foot into an Hourglass Stance. The left toes should be on a line with the middle of the right foot. Simultaneously execute a Double Over/Under Punch. The right fist should be on top of the left fist (6 inches), and both fists should be vertical.

12

Circle both hands in a clockwise manner. Slide through a left Cross Palm Block on the way to a right Outward Middle Block.

13

Execute a right Upper Cross Palm Block and a left Punch.

14

Cross step in front of the left foot with the right foot (West). Simultaneously circle both hands clockwise (Right up and left down), passing through a left Cross Palm Block to a right, Augmented, Outward Middle Ridgehand Block.

15

Pivot to the rear (South) into an Hourglass Stance. The toe of the right foot should be on a line with the middle of the left foot. simultaneously execute a left horizontal Chop and a right Lower Cross Palm Block. (Camera angle reversed)

16

Cross step in front of the right foot with the right foot (West). Simultaneously circle both hands counter clockwise (Left up and right down), passing through a right Cross Palm Block to a left, Augmented, Outward Middle Ridgehand Block. (Camera angle reversed)

17

Pivot to the rear (North) into an Hourglass Stance. The toe of the left foot should be on a line with the middle of the right foot. simultaneously execute a right horizontal Chop and a left Lower Cross Palm Block. (Camera angle normal)

18

Cross step in front of the left foot with the right foot (West). Simultaneously circle both hands clockwise (Right up and left down), passing through a left Cross Palm Block to a right, Augmented, Outward Middle Ridgehand Block. (Camera angle normal)

19

Pivot to the rear (South) into an Hourglass Stance. The toe of the right foot should be on a line with the middle of the left foot. simultaneously execute a left horizontal Chop and a right Lower Cross Palm Block. (Camera angle reversed)

20

Step back (North) with the right foot into a Back Stance (Weight right). Simultaneously swing the left hand up and clockwise in a circle to an Inverted Low Sweeping Block, and swing the right hand down and clockwise in a circle to a Cross Palm Block. (<u>Camera angle reversed</u>)

21

Step forward (South) with the left foot into a Front Stance (Weight left) and execute a left Punch. (<u>Camera angle reversed</u>)

22

Bring the right foot up to an Hourglass Stance (South) and execute a left, Augmented Upper Middle Knife Edge Block. (Camera angle reversed)

23

Step back (North) with the left foot into a Back Stance (weight left). Simultaneously execute a right Knife Edge Low Block. The left hand should be open, palm up, at the waist. (Camera angle reversed)

24

Bring the left foot to the right foot and circle both fists up and around until they are next to the body near the Tan Tien. (<u>Camera angle reversed</u>)

25

Step to the side (left/East) with the left foot into an Hourglass Stance. The left heel should be on a line with the middle of the right foot. Simultaneously Punch with both hands. (<u>Camera angle reversed</u>)

26

Bring the right foot to the left foot and circle both fists up and around until they are next to the body near the Tan Tien. (<u>Camera angle reversed</u>)

27

Step to the side (right/West) with the right foot into an Hourglass Stance. The right heel should be on a line with the middle of the left foot. Simultaneously Punch with both hands. (<u>Camera angle reversed</u>)

28

Bring the left foot to the right foot and circle both fists up and around until they are next to the body near the Tan Tien. (<u>Camera angle reversed</u>)

29

Step to the side (left/East) with the left foot into an Hourglass Stance. The left heel should be on a line with the middle of the right foot. Simultaneously Punch with both hands. (<u>Camera angle reversed</u>)

30

Pivot to the rear (North). Circle the left hand up (Clockwise) and in (Passing through a Cross Palm Block) to a Low Block. Simultaneously circle the right hand down (Counterclockwise) and in (Passing through an Inverted Sweeping Block) to a High Block. (Camera angle normal)

31

Continue the circle of the hands, passing through a left Cross Palm Block to a right Outward Middle Ridgehand Block.

32

Execute a right Cross Palm Block and a left Spear Hand. The Cross Palm Block should be above the Punch.

33

Pivot to the rear (South). Circle the right hand up (Counter Clockwise) and in (Passing through a Cross Palm Block) to a Low Block. Simultaneously circle the left hand down (Counterclockwise) and in (Passing through an Inverted Sweeping Block) to a High Block. (Camera angle reversed)

34

Continue the circle of the hands, passing through a right Cross Palm Block to a left Outward Middle Ridgehand Block. (<u>Camera angle reversed</u>)

35

Execute a left Cross Palm Block and a right Spear Hand. The Cross Palm Block should be above the Punch. (<u>Camera angle reversed</u>)

36

Pivot to the rear (North). Circle the left hand up (Clockwise) and in (Passing through a Cross Palm Block) to a Low Block. Simultaneously circle the right hand down (Counterclockwise) and in (Passing through an Inverted Sweeping Block) to a High Block. (<u>Camera angle normal</u>)

37

Continue the circle of the hands, passing through a left Cross Palm Block to a right Outward Middle Ridgehand Block.

38

Execute a right Cross Palm Block and a left Spear Hand. The Cross Palm Block should be above the Punch.

Repeat form or return to Beginning Position.

36
ACHIEVING CBM

CBM is when all parts of the body move towards the same goal at the same time.

CBM is also when there is no reaction time.

CBM is when your Intention manifests.

The Concept of CBM is tied into traditional ranking systems.

In traditional ranking systems a Shodan is a Black Belt. Sho means first, Dan means man.

Below Dan is Kyu, which means boy.

This means that when one makes the step from lower belt to Black Belt the Boy becomes a Man.

What it actually is is a statement of self, of maturation, of completed (at least on one level) Absorption of Art.

And what it means is that the body is functioning as One Unit, and therefore Intention can manifest.

It can take varying amounts of time for a person to make this statement.

The time necessary, however, can be foreshortened by understanding, at least intellectually, what you are trying to do.

And the time necessary can be foreshortened by accelerating your study of Form.

CBM comes from form permeating the body with Art.

The Form holds the Art.

By practicing your Form you assume the Form. And thereby you become Form. And Art. And CBM.

Go back and do the Forms with this concept many times before proceeding.

37
WHEN THOUGHT BECOMES ACTION

The proper way to move in the Martial Arts is to be in one position, then to be in another position, with nothing inbetween. The way to do this is to make your Thought become Action. Relax until there is no motion in any direction, have the Thought of where you will be, then let the body be in that position. Practice all your Forms and moves this way.

38
LETTING GO OF THE BODY

When you achieve CBM you will notice that you are doing the Promised Fights and your hands move by themselves. They are connected to the body, they move with complete body weight, but it is as if they are functioning by themselves. This can actually be scary, as it involves acknowledging a whole different potential of realities. I have seen a lot of people that couldn't do this, that quit the Martial Arts before they could let their body go. The ones that didn't quit, that wanted the Black Belt complete and total, were able to let this phenomena happen.

Go back and do the Forms with this concept many times before proceeding.

39
BEING WILLING

To be effective in the Martial Arts one must be willing to fight to the finish. He must be willing to do harm. And your opponent must see this in your eyes. When he does, he will not want to fight. It would be crazy, after all, for him to fight somebody who wanted to hurt him, right?

So you must be willing to hurt somebody.

But you must not hurt anybody.

If you hurt somebody your Art will die, all your hard work will go by the wayside.

It really is a cruel trick to put all this work into something, and then not be able to use it.

Of course the real gains are far beyond something as silly as fighting.

The real gains are the peace and confidence within.

The real gains are sharing that peace and confidence with others.

So remember, if you have to use your Art, then your Art has already failed.

But if you have to use your Art, make sure you are willing.

And if you are truly willing, you will never have to use your Art.

Go back and do the Forms with this concept many times before proceeding.

40
FORT APPLICATIONS

24
TRIPLE STRIKE

The Attacker kicks to the groin with the right leg.

The Defender steps back with the left leg into a Back Stance and execute a right Lower Cross Palm Block while guarding the face with a left Cross Palm Block.

The Attacker sets the right leg forward into a Front Stance and punches to the face with the left hand.

The Defender executes a right Upper Augmented Knife Hand Block.

The Attacker punches to the face with the left hand.

The Defender shuffles forward while executing a right Cross Palm Block and a left Punch to the body.

25
TWINE THROW

The Attacker steps forward with the left foot and pushes to the chest with both hands.

The Defender steps back with the left foot and executes a right Low Block and a left High Block.

The Defender continues the circling motion of the hands and twines the Attacker's arms.

The Defender steps behind the Attacker's left leg with his right leg, pushes across the chest with his right arm, and executes a Takedown.

26
QUAD STRIKE

The Attacker kicks forward with the left leg to the groin.

The Defender assumes an Hourglass Stance (weight left) and executes a right Low Block and a left High Block.

The Attacker sets the left leg forward into a Front Stance and executes a left Punch to the face.

The Defender circles the hands to execute a right Cross Palm Block.

The Attacker executes a right Punch to the body.

The Defender executes a left Outward Middle Block.

The Attacker executes a left Punch to the face.

The Defender moves the left foot forward and executes a left Cross Palm Block and a right Punch to the body.

THE ONE YEAR BLACK BELT

As I have stated, my interest is with methodology.

I have the Tight Fist my instructor taught, but I have the ways and means of countless other arts and exercises, and my interest is in how to put them all together to make a complete art. This direction of mine originally began because I became continuously bored with the Art.

People join, people quit. Not many have the patience and fortitude to achieve the True Art. Add to this the fact that I get bored with slow learners and you have a person who is interested in making a black belt faster.

The first step in making a Black Belt is to define what abilities are invested in the belt, and then decide upon what training details will give those abilities. Then you must ruthlessly and with brutal abandon discriminate against all other methods.

Unfortunately, as I described in the last chapter, most people have become too tainted for this to work.

The only reason I made Outlaw Karate work within one year was because I have a very close group of die hards. Once I went commercial it proved unworkable. People just didn't seem to have the ability to be die hard. It sounds fun, but when the work starts the weak quit.

At any rate, Outlaw Karate is put into these pages for the die hards, and if they can stick to a regular one hour a night schedule and do what I have detailed here they can achieve Black Belt in one year very, very easily. And I am not talking about shoddy belts, I am talking about Black Belts who have abilities within the Art, and can manifest those abilities.

41
1ST BROWN BELT

Science leads to prediction leads to intuition.

The material for 1st Black Belt is in the Form Dart. Dart combines the mobility of such Forms as Umbe (A variation of the Form Empi) and the foot pattern of Temple and Crane. In addition there is emphasis on the Horse Stance from such Forms as Sochin.

42
DART

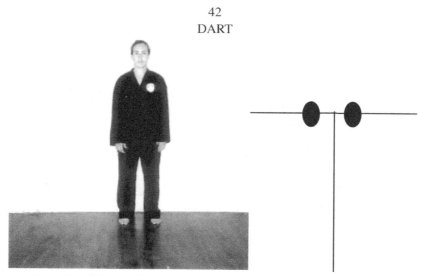

Stand in a Natural Stance facing North.

1

Step back and to the right (Southeast) with the right leg into a Horse Stance. Simultaneously execute a left Low Block and a right High Block.

131

2

Shift into a Front Stance (Weight left) and execute a left Cross Palm Block and a right Low Horizontal Spear Thrust.

3

Shift into a horse Stance. Circle the left hand counterclockwise 1 1/2 times to a Hammerfist. Circle the right hand counterclockwise one time through a parry to the hip.

4

Explode into a Front Stance (weight left). Let the right foot move shoulderwidth to the right and execute a right Punch.

5

Step forward (Northwest) with the right foot to a Crossed Stance (right foot forward-weight right). Simultaneously execute a left Punch and a right Cross Palm Block.

6

Step to the left (Southwest) with the left foot into a Horse Stance. Simultaneously execute a right Low Block and a left High Block.

7

Shift into a Front Stance (weight right) and execute a right Cross Palm Block and a left Low Horizontal Spear Thrust.

8

Shift into a horse Stance. Circle the right hand clockwise 1 1/2 times to a Hammerfist. Circle the left hand one time through a Parry and then to the hip.

9

Explode into a Front Stance (weight right). Let the left foot move shoulderwidth to the side and execute a left Punch.

10

Step forward (Northeast) with the left foot into a Crossed Stance (left foot forward-weight left). Simultaneously execute a right Punch and a left Cross Palm Block.

11

Move the right foot to the rear (North) and assume a Horse Stance. Execute a left Chop and a right High Knifehand Block. (Camera angle changes 180 degrees)

12

Move the left foot to the left (face Southeast) into a Front Stance (weight left). Simultaneously execute a left Cross Palm Block and a right Low Horizontal Spear Thrust. (Camera angle reversed)

13

Pull the left foot back and assume a Back Stance (weight right). Simultaneously circle the left hand counterclockwise 1 1/2 times to an Outward Middle Block. Circle the right hand one time through a Parry then to the hip. (Camera angle reversed)

14

Move the right foot forward (Southeast) on line with the left heel. Point the right foot at the left foot and execute a right Horizontal Elbow Strike. (Camera angle reversed)

15

Move the right foot forward (Southeast) into a Front Stance (weight right). Simultaneously execute a left Punch. (Camera angle reversed)

16

Replace the right foot with the left foot and execute a right Front Snap Kick and a right Cross Palm Block. (Camera angle reversed)

17

Replace the left foot with the right foot, slide the left foot back to where it was in position 15 (Front stance-weight right). Simultaneously execute a left Punch. (Camera angle reversed)

18

Move the right foot back and then to the right (Southwest) into a Front Stance (weight right). Simultaneously execute a right Cross Palm Block and a left Low Horizontal Spear Thrust. (Camera angle reversed)

19

Bring the right foot back to a Back Stance (weight left). Circle the right hand Clockwise 1 1/2 times to an Outward Middle Block. Circle the left hand one time through a Parry then to the hip. (Camera angle reversed)

20

Move the left foot forward (Southwest) until it is on a line with the right heel and pointing at the right foot. Simultaneously execute a left Horizontal Elbow Strike. (<u>Camera angle reversed</u>)

21

Step forward (Southwest) with the left foot into a Front Stance (weight left). Simultaneously execute a right Punch. (<u>Camera angle reversed</u>)

22

Replace the left foot with the right foot and execute a left Front Snap Kick and left Cross Body Palm Block. (Camera angle reversed)

23

Replace the right foot with the left foot, slide the right foot back to where it was in position 21 (Front stance-weight left). Simultaneously execute a right Punch. (Camera angle reversed)

24

Step to the rear (East) with the right foot into a Horse Stance. Execute a right Chop and a left High Knifehand Block. (<u>Camera angle normal</u>)

Repeat the form or return to the beginning position.

43
PROMOTIONAL REQUIREMENTS

It's only fair to tell you what I look for when I promote somebody. I look for relaxation. When a person is relaxed speed will come naturally, the techniques will flow effortlessly, and 'Think' is at a minimum. When a person is relaxed he will do the Forms without thinking and Intention will manifest. Applications will be done zip zip zip without needing to think or otherwise refer to memory. When a person is relaxed he will execute his level of Freestyle easily and without confusion.

There really is nothing mysterious or mystical about this. A person either knows his material, or he doesn't. When he does he is relaxed, and I promote.

Go back and do the Forms with this concept many times before proceeding.

44
THE CREATION OF ART

The 1st Brown student is expected to create applications from the From Dart for his test to Black Belt.

Creation is the bring into existence of something new.

Art is the expression of self.

Some people hold that one should never change a training method, a Form, an application, etc.

But one must change. One must change in a moment in the middle of a fight. One must create movement as the need arises. So to say that change is not allowed is foolishness of the worst kind.

There is one rule, however, that must be adhered to when creating Art. That rule is one of function. Never change your Art for something that doesn't work. I have done my best to enhance the Martial Arts by increasing scientific understanding of their function. I have tried to phrase rules of Energy and Physics and Mechanics and so on. These rules invariably pertain to function, and they will never change. They may, however, become better understood.

Incidentally, there is one little pitfall that you must be aware of. Some people change the Art when they cannot make it work. This is another example of supreme foolishness. If the weakness is in the Art, change the Art. If the weakness is in the person, change the person. The trick is to be honest enough with yourself to understand where the weakness is.

Go back and do the Forms with this concept many times before proceeding.

45
HORSE MEDITATION

In Horse Meditation one sits in a very deep horse Stance, the buttocks as low as the tops of the knees. One arm is in a Knifehand High Block. The other arm is extended to the side with a reverse 'Chicken Beak' (Also: 'Little Fist,' 'Whip,' and so on) pointing to the rear. The head is turned towards the Chicken Beak and the eyes are on the closed tips of the fingers.

The idea is to concentrate upon the fingertips so hard that you do not feel the pain. One should be able to sit in this position for an hour. I have found that it helps if one concentrates on breathing to the Tan Tien and not resisting the floor. Ultimately, where you put your Intention is up to you. The most important thing to realize is that the pain will not hurt you, and that you have the ability to surmount any pain. In short, if you think of pain you get pain., if you think of what you are doing you get what you are doing. If you stay in the position long enough the pain will cease.

Go back and do the Forms with this concept many times before proceeding.

46
JUSTIFYING YOUR EXISTENCE

The common belief is that it takes three to four years to reach Black Belt.
Furthermore, it takes ten to twelve years to Master.
And it takes three lifetimes to understand.
Well, that may be fine for cavemen, but...
In 1908 Yatsune Itosu, a 'Grandfather' of Karate, made the statement, 'One to two hours of training every day for three to four years will make you Master Karate.'
So a hundred years ago it didn't take ten years, but three to four.
What happened in the last hundred years to make Karate harder? Or man weaker?
What happened is that every single person who studied and taught Karate felt that he had to justify his (her?) existence. They did this by expanding the Teachings.
Sure, some of the stuff that was contributed was valuable.
But a lot wasn't. And a lot was nothing more than adding to the confusion.
I observed this phenomena in the style of Karate I was taught. And I observed this phenomena taking place with every teacher of Karate I came across.
In this day and age of advanced communications, with the advent of books and videos and jets and phones and such it is very easy to become overloaded with data. And this glut of knowledge becomes manifest in the various expanded systems.
What I have done is take everything out. I kicked out everything single thing I could and I boiled everything down to basics and made lists and tried to formulate the information on the lists into systems of workable knowledge.
The result is that a Black Belt can be earned within a year very easily. (Please understand that Itosu's reference to one to two hours of training every day is very valid.)
And Karate can be mastered in three to four years very, very easily.
As a matter of fact it can be mastered within a couple of years. Of course Mastery comes faster the more one trains.
And, as a matter of fact, the entire field of the Martial Arts can be Mastered within three to four years.
The trick is to understand the concepts, not to just robotically follow instructions and have Boot Camp workouts. And with this statement I have come to the heart of this little discourse.
Don't justify your existence by altering my Art.

Don't change the Art because you can't make it work.

I like the idea of achieving the goal of the Martial Arts within a short period of time. Furthermore, I have no intention of spending three or four lifetimes trying to understand the Martial Arts. One will do nicely, thank you.

Go back and do the Forms with this concept many times before proceeding.

47
TESTS

Following are the written tests I gave throughout the system to make sure that the student had the knowledge and wasn't just looking good. I had to make sure that the student understood, exactly, everything that he was doing, or else the whole system would have been meaningless.

Can you pass the following tests?

GREEN BELT TEST

Student being tested: Date:

1) What is the purpose of the Martial Arts?
2) What is CBM?
3) What is Focus?
4) What is grounding?
5) What is Body Alignment?
6) When do you breath out?
7) When do you breath in?
8) What is the Injury Formula?
9) Why should a body be relaxed?
10) What is 'Joy of Combat' and why should it be avoided?

GREEN/BROWN BELT TEST

Student being tested: Date:

1) Why are the Martial Arts a microcosm of life?
2) What are the Three Levels of the Martial Arts?
3) Define the First Level.
4) Define the Second Level.
5) Define the Third Level.
6) What are the Three Essential Ingredients?
7) Describe how the Energy Formula works.
8) What are the Six Distances?
9) Describe the Force/Flow Formula.
10) If a student gets promoted he becomes a bigger_____.

3RD BROWN BELT TEST

Student being tested: Date:

1) What is a Closed Combat System?
2) Where is the body constructed from?
3) What are the Five Basic Arm Positions and how is Energy used in them?
4) What are the Four Basic Arm Geometries?
5) What are the Six Basic Arm Directions?
6) What are the Three Components of Power?
7) What are the Three Stages of Promised Fights?
8) What does one do beyond Three Strike Block and Counter?
9) What are the Four Stages of Freestyle?
10) What is the Secret of One Way Freestyle?

2ND BROWN BELT TEST

Student being tested: Date:

1) Why is a Brown Belt so dangerous and what should he do about it?
2) Without_____there is no Art.
3) Describe the Secret of Power.
4) How should you view pain?
5) How do you overcome what you can't face?
6) What is the Art composed of?
7) What are the Five Stages of Pain?
8) What is life divided into?
9) What does a True Martial Artist make a practice of doing?
10) How does the footwork of Crane and Temple differentiate from that of Moon?

1ST BROWN BELT TEST

Student being tested: Date:

1) Do you see yourself as wearing a Black Belt?
2) What do Temple and Crane sum up?
3) What do Moon and Fort sum up?
4) CBM is when all parts of the body do what?
5) How does CBM relate to reaction time?
6) When you CBM what will manifest?
7) A boy becomes a man by making a statement of_____.

8) How does Thought become Action?

9) What is the phenomena of 'Letting Go of the Body?'

10) To be effective in the Martial Arts one must be willing to do what?

1ST BLACK BELT TEST

Student being tested: Date:

1) What does the color of a White Belt mean?

2) What does the color of a Green Belt mean?

3) What does the color of a Brown Belt mean?

4) What does the color of a Black Belt mean?

5) What should a person do after achieving Black Belt?

6) What is the pitfall in 'Creation of Art?'

7) What happened in the last 100 years to make man weaker, or Karate harder?

8) What is happening to time in Hi-Lo?

9) When does somebody get promoted?

10) What is the difference between an Expert and a Master and what are the Three Steps to becoming a Master?

CONCLUSION

The color Black signifies nothing. A Black Belt, instead of thinking he knows everything, realizes that he has just scratched the surface. In fact, he has started to come to grips with just how little he does know.

The next step, after Black Belt, is to become Master. There are three steps necessary to becoming a Master.

The first step is to continue your study of Karate. Now that you know it you must Polish it.

The second step is to learn the softer side of the Martial Arts, that side of the Art dealing with controlling another individual so that neither he nor yourself nor anybody else comes to harm.

While there is an Art to Destruction, the True Art is in Control.

The Third step is to learn how to teach. There is a vast difference between the knowledge you now possess, and the knowledge necessary to a Teacher. A Teacher has a unique 'Third Person' viewpoint of the Arts. This viewpoint is essential for your further progress.

You don't really know something until you have taught it.

Congratulations on becoming Expert in Karate.

Continue.

Pan Gai Noon is the connection between Kung Fu and Okinawan Karate. In this volume you will find a complete dissertation, including the most significant forms, of this magnificent Martial Art.

Pan Gai Noon is available at Amazon.

You may also find more information concerning it on either MonsterMartialArts.comn, or AlCaseBooks.com.

Buddha Crane Karate is one of the first books ever written on Matrixing a Martial Art. It is a very important work, as it shows how Matrixing develops within the creation of art.

Buddha Crane Karate is available at Amazon.

You may also find more information concerning Buddha Crane Karate on either MonsterMartialArts.comn, or AlCaseBooks.com.

Kwon Bup American Karate showcases the forms developed by Sensei Robert J. Babich, and the black belts of the Kang Duk Won.

Sensei Babich is the only American to ever master 'The One Finger Trick,' which is to thrust a finger through a board not break it, but to leave a hole.

Kwon Bup American Karate is available at Amazon.

You may also find more information concerning Buddha Crane Karate on either MonsterMartialArts.comn, or AlCaseBooks.com.

Karate to Shaolin to Pa Kua Chang contains three short manuals containing training forms, two man forms, drills and other material. This is designed to take the student from the hard knuckles of Karate to the softer Chi Gung 'internal' practices of Kung Fu.

The books are not an esoteric blast of words, but rather concise forms and techniques. Thus, the student is encouraged not just to talk the talk, but to walk the actual path of martial arts progression.

Karate to Shaolin to Pa Kua Chang is available at Amazon.

You may also find more information concerning thisbook on either MonsterMartialArts.comn, or AlCaseBooks.com.

About the Author

Al Case began the martial arts in 1967. Since that time he has studied Kenpo, Karate, Northern Shaolin, Southern Shaolin, Wing Chun, Tai Chi Chuan, Pa Kua Chang, and more.

He became a writer for the magazines in 1981, and had his own column (Case Histories) in Inside Karate.

He has written dozens of books and produced many video courses on the martial arts.

He has written well over two million words on the martial arts, which makes him the most prolific martial arts writer of all time.

He is the creator of Matrixing (the first real science of the martial arts) and Neutronics (A unique Martial Arts philosophy).

Interested students can view his work at MonsterMartialArts.com and AlCaseBooks.com, and others of his websites.

Currently, he lives on a mountain top in Southern California where he is building a martial arts temple.

Made in the USA
Las Vegas, NV
29 October 2023